DEATH

AT SEA

Death at Sea

POEMS

YOUSSEF ALAOUI-FDILI

Paper Press

DEATH AT SEA Poems
Youssef Alaoui-Fdili
Some of these poems first appeared in *Exquisite Corpse, Cherry Bleeds, If & When,* and *Carcinogenic Poetry*
Ocean, skeleton, interior art circles by
Rachael Winn Yon of Los Osos, CA
Cover collage, book design
Youssef Alaoui-Fdili
All content herein copyright December 2013
Paper Press Books & Assoc. Publishing Co.
ISBN 10: 978-0615915739
ISBN 13: 0615915736

A PAPER PRESS BOOK.

To my Family.

Whenever I find myself growing grim about the mouth; whenever it is a damp, drizzly November in my soul; whenever I find myself involuntarily pausing before coffin warehouses, and bringing up the rear of every funeral I meet; and especially whenever my hypos get such an upper hand of me, that it requires a strong moral principle to prevent me from deliberately stepping into the street, and methodically knocking people's hats off—then, I account it high time to get to sea as soon as I can. This is my substitute for pistol and ball.

—Herman Melville, Moby Dick

CONTENTS

DEATH AT SEA

POEMS

PREFACE

I loved my continent. I built it and lived on it. Then eventually, I tired of it. I left everything. I took to a new place. I loved my new land. I invested in it, but it did not suit me. This lasted many years.

I discovered that I was made for yet another place altogether. This epiphany brought me to the sea, knowing that my home was between continents, belonging everywhere and nowhere simultaneously, missing everyone I'd ever known.

I came to acknowledge that I was welcomed by a certain kind of people and not a location, and that their place was everywhere, for they could be found anywhere and everywhere, populating the most interesting cracks and spaces of the world, often ignored by others.

This book was not written in a single voice but in many, each from a similar standpoint: At sea, far from everything, a quiet moment to write one's thoughts, in the belly of a ship, drifting the heights of separation anxiety; enigma of the human condition.

A Sea Too Bright

In sum,
the entire splashy glass horizon
holds its breath for a moment
when the memory of your face
resurfaces.

As so,
the very edges of nature
shudder and retract at the idea
of your voice, now gone.

Lost to the wind,
reminding us souls to wish
for a self less brittle than porcelain
and a keepsake less persistent.

Arcades of sky fall open
to permit the iota of you
to return,
tipping at the edge,
and speak with me, hot-faced; alone.

The sea today is too bright
yet, I must look away from the ship
to interrupt my thoughts
or reflect again your earthy shore.

Again Tonight Swimming

Skies are vast and oblivious
my mind circles its tiny case,
shoulders of Orion stretching.
I am lost once more,
treading the icy black horns
of a boundless ocean.

Date palms slope
in memory, a pleasanter time.
Seals bark on the rocks.
I keep waking here
a few yards from the ship.

There is nothing darker
or more unconcerned
than the waters around me,
a blank surface reaching everywhere
to the empty horizon.

Again tonight, I
find myself swimming.
Each time, this flotsam
considers itself either worthy
or not, of climbing back
up over the rails.

Crush of Daylight

Close on the tail of #27 by J.S.

A clear stainless sea of blood
still crashes relentlessly
against the rocks
where our veiled skeletons
teetered and sang to the sun.

The jetty trembled
beneath us even then
when our song grew to howling
as the sky, a rolling blue brow
and the sun, a dazzling third eye
plastered us to the foot
of the volcano heart

until the crush
of daylight subsided
and smoky colors rose
behind the shifting mist
finally releasing its grip.

It was then we witnessed
the harbor bow
to receive the weight
of evening tides.

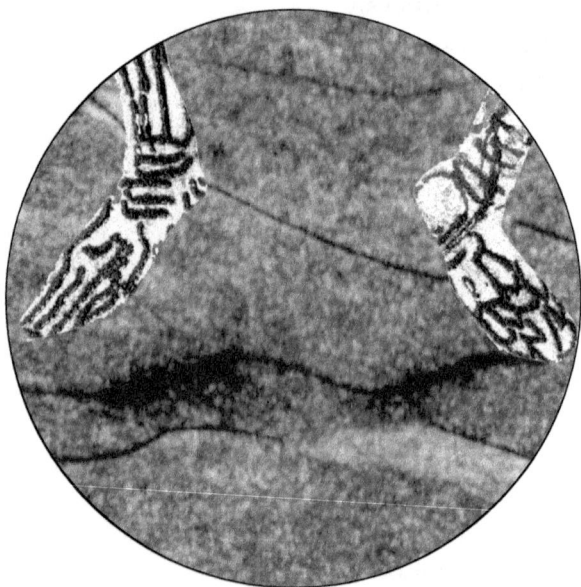

Dinghy Song

To murmur while hanging sails

Skins we hang in time so dear
saving wounds were never ours
loving warm and overheard
holding on to a land so far.

If it's a knife you need it's over here
and tell us why you've come this way
the shiniest one is yours to keep
away we fly and go along.

But it's far too low in salty mud
and away we fly and go along
our naked lives we cancel now
the enemy is the one we build.

There's gold for them that hurts
and mine is always pouring
for I'm drunk again my dear
so my heart flies and so we go.

And if this song is nowhere heard
then I will be one nearest to you.

Away we fly and so we go.
Away we fly and on and on.

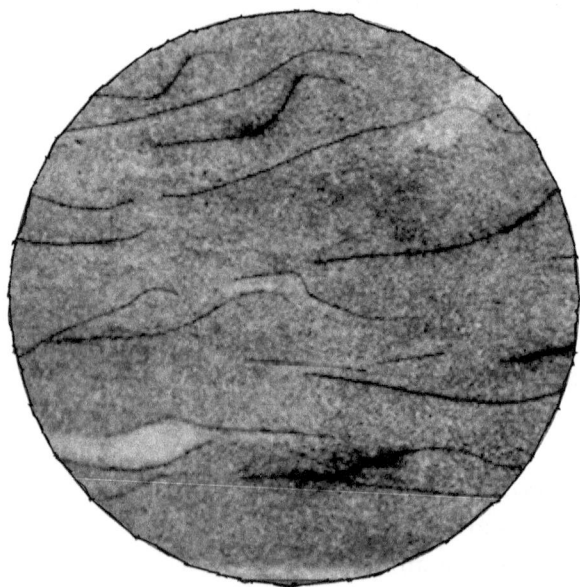

Drowning

Parting the smooth silt
of your undercurrent

Dabbling your liquid soils
your firm crescent fish

Toiling bare
through your unlit depths

Tangled within your swaying ivies

Sun filters over
your dappling curvature

I am engaged

Swilling it all
not asking for air.

Ecstasy of Barr Lassiter

Herons bask
on the tiled dome
of your universe.

Their shadows wait
in dim pools
at their feet.

When the sun
sets fire among old twigs
and tangerine clouds,
this too is a sea.

Your family sits silent
dotted with barnacles.
Your mother stares
into an empty fireplace.

The birds and I then realize
any sea would be home
for you.

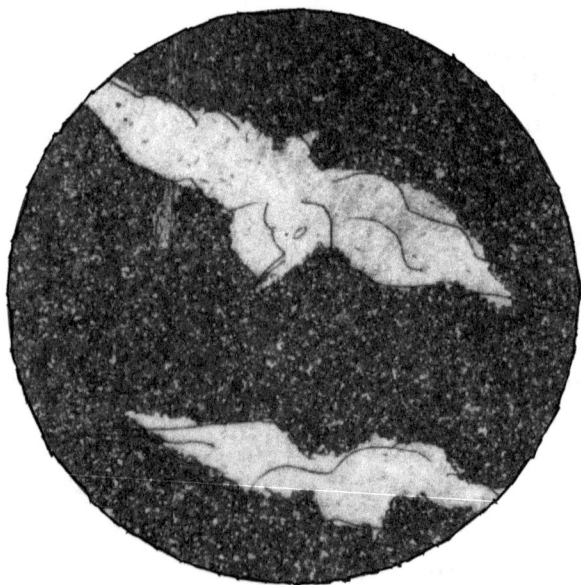

Here, Birdless

A cast in the sand
framed by several stones
betrays the print of a bird.

It skipped here and left.
Running now back to its horde
it was a collector. A tinker. A soul.

Here on shore, we find
secrets of the deep
splayed flat by currents.

Undiscovered jewel box
of careless non-involvement.

Power enough to carve mountains.
Power enough to leave us
stranded here, birdless.

I Have Seen the Dead
Seal Body Rising

I.
I have seen the dead seal body
rising and falling with the current.
It heaves to escape its auburn rug
floating lopsided; face hidden
entrails migrating into the water
like man o' war tendrils.

In my dreams it hovers in the air like a saint
abdomen sliced cleanly like church doors
viscera issuing like Sunday goers
how pleasant it would have been
back then, to hold your hand.

I see the love in your body
the dreamy god set deep within your brow
a solemn prayer meant for someone like me
brimming with hope and fire
and we no more than companions.
It is there I wait
listening forever.

II.
In my mind
your body soars endless waterways
as spirits carry you unguided
haunting the bulwarks of your skeleton.
To me, you are nothing less
than a savior.

In my heart
I am a child trapped rotting in memory
crying for hours
my leg slung through the floorboard
of our hideaway
waiting for someone to find me.

In my soul
you are the ends of the eyes
the pall of the wake
the bringer of rot
the kindliest siren.

I have seen the dead seal body
rising and falling with the current.
It will be
the last thing that I see.

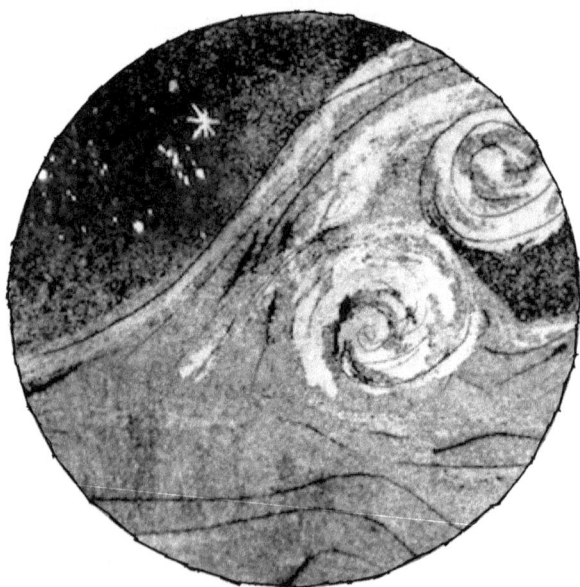

Love at Sea with John Reed, May 1916

Damnable oceans erupt and swallow
  entire schooners; leaving not a sign of them.
  Shrouding black-blue canyons
trimmed by thick froth
  form biting teeth as I have witnessed immense
      vessels overwhelmed–
Grander is the purveyance
of your lips upon my body.

Dour and convoluted skies
bearing loads of rain, vaulting
  ten furlongs, tread the water's surface
  on flashing spindly legs of molten iron; the seas'
  snow-tipped caps are drawn upward
a fathom at a time
      urging to caress the belly
of ruptured bleating clouds.
Such commotion only presses us closer
against one another.

From obliterating voluminous leagues stretch blind
  wavering tentacles, bleached luminescent, grasping
    at skimming hulls to nourish
on the human life putty.
I am less than I was; more than I will become.
    You are effete yet vital.

Last night I cried to God
  and God cried back over his steaming tisane
    of licorice spiked with mescal.
  I wailed at him in pain for having cast me upon
    these 'scapes
  and he slid the ship's planks from my feet and
  across my back and cracked my head against the
mainmast.
    Such unforgiving dialogue!
But I will not ungive the parlance of your body against
mine!

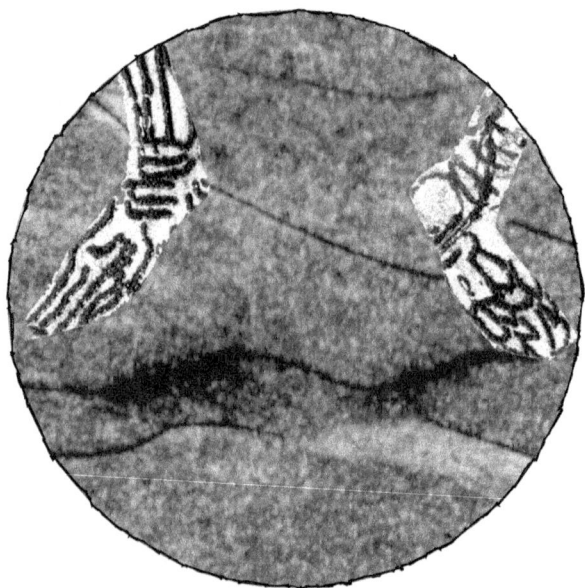

Muscular Tentacles

Thin bubbles rising
my neck and face
pulse with pressure
in the ringing silence.

The behemoth has risen
wrapping around me.
Some maiden's fantasy
has me in headlock!

My eyes are bulging
mouth clamped shut
these arms are no good
I'm quietly fading.

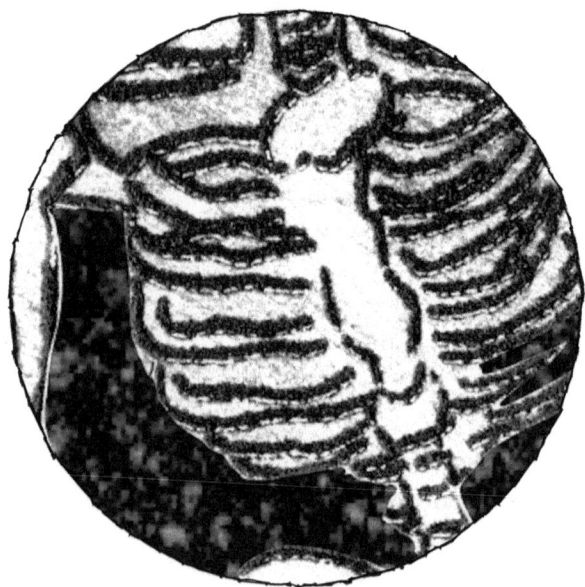

On The Passing Of My Ship-Brother.

Black angels dance
on shoulders of the air
the Ocean pikes in grey
mounds about the ship.

Sky horses roll their eyes
in fear, bridles speckled
with froth. Death lurches
above, deep in the clouds.

A memory stands in my vision.
It is a black, oily, floating stone
edifice, spraying plumes
at the sea. Its mist reaches the ship.

Light bends around it
twisting into forms familiar
and repulsive, wrapping
my attention and pulling me.

Hot tears stream down my face.
I never meant to let you die,
Ship-Brother.
You trusted me with your life.

Planks of the deck wheeze
and flex, letting the sea
have its way with them.
Our troubles are shared.

Ship-Brother
it is difficult to maintain
my temper when I remember
the two of us.

This song intones our doom.
Sky horses bleed into the Ocean.
We are lonely, rotting, destitute.
I never meant to kill you.
I had only hoped to save you.

Paean for Hassan Sabbah

I am the country sun.
I am the ambivalence of open spaces.
I am the haste in mountain breezes.
I am the heavy force, the rushing crest
of saltwater horizons.

I am the trouble with hearts.
Doubting the casements of your ribcage
I leap from it, into the sky
and there among the clouds
I leave a single, indelible, bloody hoof print.

I am the bending canvas, the enriching blue ocean
the marching pavement sky.
Any world beyond this is still within my scope
for I hold the glass which allows the readings of
galaxies.

I am the lens itself; the bearer withal.
The compass proves nothing.
None escapes my route, for I am every pathway.
Every passageway.

My iron tongue is vaulted at its core and houses the
stories of a thousand richly decorated bibles, telling the
composite fabric of infinitely intersecting human
fables and histories.

For I am the dead.
And at your gates I wait for you and I pull the trigger
of me to die into you.
Unfolded thus, I am wishing the silver
cannons of your gaze
would pummel and flatten my obnoxious
and muddy heart.
For I am the melted.
So let the poison darts of your eyes
slip in softly to my temples
and carry me, tumbling, deep into the sand.
Mixing under, let me graft my body to the roots of
palms and fern trees, and, suckled up through the veins
of the trees, push me out again as a nut or a fruit, so
burdened with my dedication to you, that I again drop
to the earth and melt rapidly, deeply into its environs,
flowing endlessly with the subterranean cosmos.

At peace, I again ride the currents of lava
up through the strata,
and bursting the crust of the earth
I am a giant spray of orange.
My cloud darkens the sun.
I destroy the continent.

My body rains blobs of scorching lava all over you, and
you are now a city.
Your people are your soul, and your memory of me
is a box.

Your land is destroyed. At last my love is proven.
The house around the box is encased in stone.
There are seven steps leading down to a window.
I crush the roof of your city.
It falls under the ocean.
I'm sorry I killed you.
And I wake up crying.
The lake is an eye, but whose?
It lies unblinking in the canyon.

Pointed—
That Beam of Light

That beam of light upon your face
reveals the blush of summer gone from it.
And now, treatment for a reflective era:

Evening.
She creeps over the trees
and valleys on multiple legs
of brittle iron poles.

An expanding barracks
not fluttering
but oozing in mile-high wafts
and we pointed toward her
hurtled into the East.

Emerging evening;
a cold blanket with rusted edges,
replacing daylight
with a fickle promise in dreams.

Instead,
she fills the sleeping gulf
with ideas of living acts
never committed, never actualized,
hardly remembered.

Finally alone,
this is the river we speak to—
Grey, broad, shallow, leafless, birds leaving it,
and bridged.
An expanse best fled from.
A kept secret. A mute response.

And from above
the sirens spiral around it,
just beyond the periphery
lies your rock island,
a glowing carnelian outpost.
The final gateway to spring.

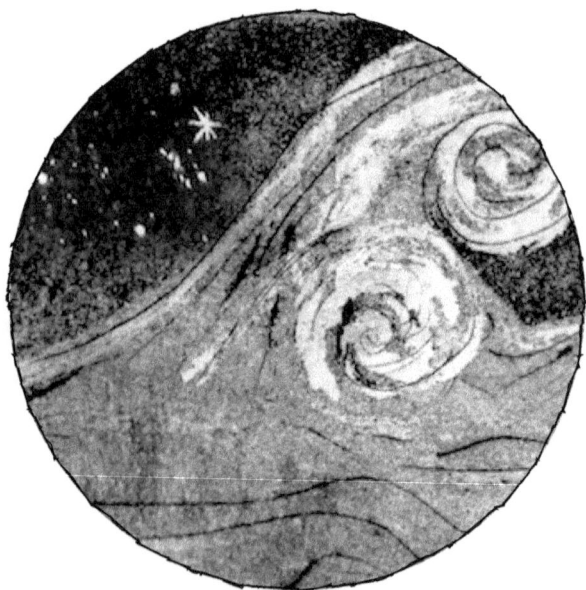

Praise!

The sea froth juts its speckled fist!
A thousand arms spread
over clay-stacked cliffs
soldiering off the land.

A multitude of tireless forms
all reaching and erasing
wiping away at the conscience
forcing back the past

with sweeping gestures
consuming and belching it.
Who were we anyway?
Too embarrassed to remember.

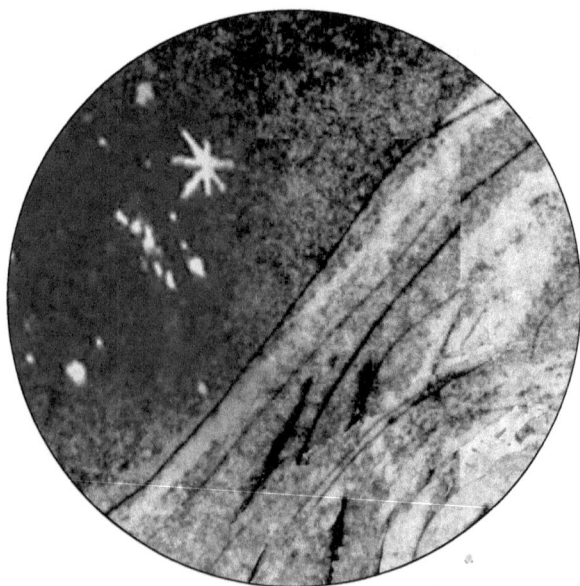

The Precipice

Broad canopy of night
enshrouds this jagged rock
that calls me forward

stars twist above
tear at my skull in silence

I plod the stones
until my vision heeds
the horizon wrapping

steep ribbons of clay beneath me
evening's events softly turning
muffled by the shuddering sea

with a sigh, it wonders
when I'll throw myself into it
scaly back of ocean rolling

lips and teeth continually gnashing
I consider my last sentence spoken
strong medicines slide through my blood

they pulse in my head, exposing my circuitry
full bore to the night
I couldn't climb back down if I had to.

Pym's Song

Trapped within a fortress of boxes
suffocating to write this
a glowing candle stump saps my oxygen.

I can only watch in stupor
as the swells tip and rumble
outside my porthole.

I am awake again,
deep in the frigate hull
parched and sickened.

For company, the stench of my dead dog's body.

Past the noise of stamping feet above
and the creaking wooden pit that surrounds me
are the gasps and groans
of chanting demons, wheezing dour airs
intoning madness, agony, and deceit.

They rob the final bits of my memory.
My trust in a liar has buried me here.
The crew laughs at my predicament.

*To this ruinous melody will I slide my painful
bag of bones headlong into silent, thundering sleep.*

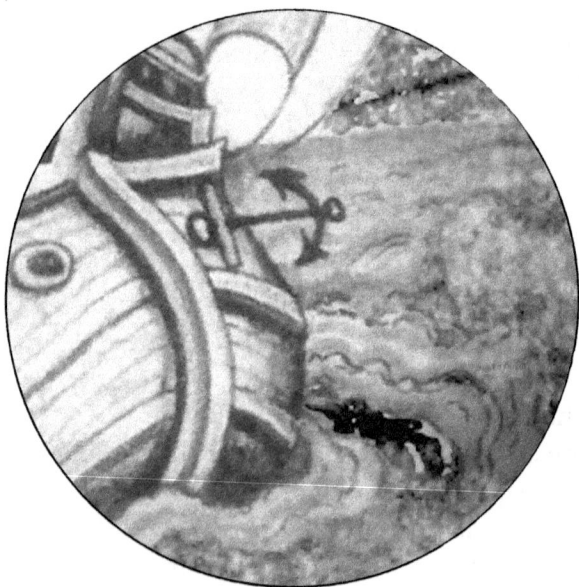

Reflection

Gentle are the twisting tides.
Boiling and heaving, folding in pressure,
awesome tanks of deep gather overhead
to foster meager thoughts.

Here among the sea crags,
struggling past scattered ideas
dull glitter in the quivering light,
have I made my home.

A summons, a broken cry,
from the sheltering density,
a meek and penetrating voice
has brought me here to drift.

I cannot hear it nor can I stop listening.
The message is lost.
I tumble unguided, swept over mute valleys,
obscure mountains and maligned seabeds.

Every nook and cave hurling darkness,
at once roaring but elusive

penetrating but empty
every one of them passing.

Suddenly the fathoms ease
and a single coin spirals toward me.
Far above, a black elliptic hull
barely treads the water surface.

It's my own face peering over the side
a pale speck, shifting, tilting
following the coin
dropped into its reflection.

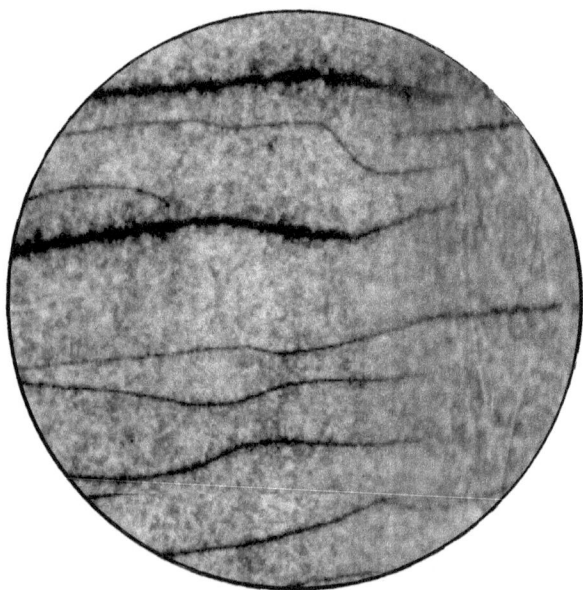

Scurvy

My sheets are dry
my feet are clouds.

I am an oblique invalid
and I am empty.

The clock is immobile
my blankets are failing.

Reading is boring
the door is a tower
This sea is a haven.

I'm resting and dying
I roam the windows
Even the glass is framed.

I can only see sky
At times birds are in it
They ignore me and pass.

The clock has forgotten
My head is a burden.

My legs are wooden
And my feet are clouds.

The Search For Shore

In the end
it is always ever blinded
we pulling on oars or swimming
barrel-chested and shivering
reaching, yet hurled ever further.

In the end
hidden within the foaming drapery
we are scant, brittle, bodiless
children pretending to be insects
floating in the weed.

Shipwrecked

Awakened from a dream
hiding in the dunes from my shipmates
after courtship with an island lass
then fallen into slumber
among day open flowers.

Her perfume upon me
The sea shouldn't look this way,
said a voice.
The water won't flow right,
it said.

Rubbing at the sleepy blur
I saw waves leaving the shore
the sea became an arching dome
perfume and flowers had vanished.

I held my face in disbelief
as if something was watching me
I thew a rock into the water
but the rock leapt back
and knocked me solid in the chest.

I fell to the ground
the sky spread black wings overhead
squeezing down upon me
I waited for death, yet I could not die
I gasped for air.

The skiff had overturned above me
and the ship, wild in flames
screams and jetsam everywhere
yet I was protected; I swam to shore
to escape my dream at last!

Was it you, fair dune maid
held me down in the sage
and reversed the tides
to beach me here, lonely and withered?
I will not thank you for saving me.

Sons of Devils

The crow flies over the fields milord
the melons are fat in the furrow
and we are richer for autumn has touched us again.

The hay is rolled in the field milord
the plow is made ready for harvest
and we are nothing but sons of devils again.

The storm clouds are stacked on the mountain
the leaves are golden in the arbor
and the grapes are heavy with sugar.

The soldiers are all dead in the grass milord
the sunflowers cry to the soil
and we are nothing but sons of devils again.

Now who was the one who promised a fair life
and who was the one who told her to wait
and we are nothing but stubborn liars again.

The ribbons she bought for her wedding have faded
the flowers she bought for her funeral are dry
but no one remembers the widow.

Her man is watching from his place in the sky
she won't notice him touching her shoulder
and we are nothing but sons of devils again.

The crow flies over the fields milord
the melons are fat in the furrow
and we are richer for autumn has touched us again.

The storm clouds are stacked on the mountain
the sunflowers cry to the soil
and we are nothing but sons of devils.

The Standing Brig

On a bright summer day
ten degrees North of Capricorn
our vessel hit a ramp
of slow moving water.

The temperature below decks
was a moorish steam bath
when our captain yelled "Sculls!"
And we each grabbed our oars.

We dripped down to the planks
and pulled forward mightily
but the vessel wouldn't budge.
As the kelp spun around us

"Damn it if we're not
caught in a forest!"
The captain's eyes moved about him
plotting our destiny.

"The currents below
are forcing us back."
And truth he had spoken.
The last of us trembling

for no one had ever
seen such a disaster.
Miles from nowhere
a giant eddy turning clockwise

faced us down in our path
and was ever determined
to guide us to its middle.
Trim fingers of kelp

darkly outlined its surface
each rising and sinking,
tracing the circle.
"We're never leaving this hell hole!"

Somebody muttered
and the rest of us clambered
topside to view.
What it was, was immense

with ripples and valleys
I'd have mistaken it for land
had it not been so glassy.
Like a thinking creature

with wings and a nest
was just below surface
and wanted to digest us.
"We're lost. We'll never see home,"

Said another one next to me.
"We've not begun trying!"
Said our captain, with hope.
"Grab the kerosene, grab the rum

but leave some for later
we'll need it to wait out
the rest of the voyage.
I need you and you!

Take the barrels
and pour them overboard
but gently; so it floats
all the way to the middle!"

And so it was done
although doubtful at first
the fuel was dispensed with
over the moorings.

"And now…!" as he gestured,
evening settling.
The sun at an angle
lit the liquid floating.

It made an oily trail
spiraling inward
to the core of the nest.
"Once we burn up these weeds

we'll have traction and haste!
We'll make our way out
of this nagging current!"
And we looked around stupefied

for what was his plan
but to burn submerged kelp
to free us from sacrifice.
Yet what could we do

for the weeds had us locked
and the eddy was permanent
we had to try something.
"Let's just use a lifeboat.

we can leave the ship
where she lies.
I've got nothing important
locked up in my quarters…"

That's what they said
but our captain was a bold one
bent on taking us
to the East Indies or die.

Die is more likely
when I considered
how a sea set aflame
would likely consume us.

"Now get me a match!"
Hollered our captain
and each of us felt
our pockets for a box.

The first mate next to him
handed a mug-sized cannon
loaded with a charge
used for signaling.

With a word or two beforehand
and the captain nodding
he aimed for the outer ring
of the oily spiral.

Beneath, the dark hands
of the forest
raised and lowered.
Only an inkling belied

the density beneath.
We each held our breath.
Someone began singing
a song he knew

for events gone bad.
The captain fired
with an ear-shredding fizz.
The missile landed

at the edge of the spiral.
A second had passed
but the charge was alight
when it skipped on the surface

and started the fire.
"Look alive ye dogs!"
He said like a champion.
Each of us gaping

off the starboard rigging.
Evening was setting
and the conflagration grew.
We all watched in horror

as the kelp forest boiled.
At times it flew at us
at others it groaned.
It writhed in pain.

It begged us for mercy.
The fire spread sideways
and came for the ship
but the captain had lowered

a team tight to aft
to pour water on the hull
and fend off the flames.

A blister beneath
the sea was rising;
a glowing lump of char
festering at us.

The first mate mentioned
to the captain beside him

"It's a pocket of methane, sir."
A man of the books, he was.
"A pocket of what!"
"The layers of earth, under the water

have a solid deposit
of crystalline fuel
locked up inside them.
That must be what's driving

the spiraling current!"
"Crystalline fuel!
Dear God. If you're right,
we'll be nothing but ashes

as soon as she blows!"
But none of us heard him
because the sight
was so frightening.

It seemed like the ocean
was madly scrambling

to pull us all under
courtesy of the devil himself.

The waters around us
were lit like a canopy.
An explosion flew up
dwarfing the mainmast

showering pebbles
back to the surface.
Some hit the fires
and popped up again.

They flew off like meteors
into the night.
But some just bobbled
across the deck.

It was curious
and suddenly interesting
in light of the catastrophe.
Some people kicked them

from underfoot
as the decks were listing.
They exploded on impact
and blew off their toes

shredding their boots
like so much wet paper.

"Take care with that debris!"
Said the captain, wryly.

One man was shrieking.
His arms outstretched
face raised to heaven
and God help the fellow.

He'd caught one in his mouth.
When the pebble ignited
it turned his face inside out.

His bellows just petered
to a noise like a foghorn.
"Throw that man over!"
said our faith-loving captain.

"And get our brooms topside
and the strongest below!
We've got a mountain of rowing
to do before sunrise!"

So away went the screamer
and up came the brooms
and down went my team
and I was among them.

We rowed until dawn
till our bodies were noodles
but we never stopped pulling.

There was a point

where we even
forgot where we sat.
Two men died rowing
but their arms kept on moving

and the sun had returned
to bake overhead.
The fire showed no signs of abating.
The swirling masses

of kelp kept on churning.
We forgot where we were
and left our bodies.
I had a vision.

I was pacing a forest.

I swam to the edge
and found myself hugging
the toes of the highest
peaks in the land.

Birds had roosted
on top of my head
mistaking my locks
for the branches of trees.

The forest swayed
to the breeze of my breath.
The nature around me
was lifting and sustaining.

I trudged my way
to the top of the peak.
My wife and daughter
floated in front of me.

They wanted to sing in unison
a prayer for wind
I knew the song
they were supposed to be singing

and as they opened
their mouths to begin
an explosion occurred
inside the boat.

One of the pebbles
had fallen to the floor.
An oarsman then
reached down to grab it

and in an effort
to soothe his pain
he took the ultimate remedy
by slapping the token

hard against his forehead.
He screamed for an instant
and sprayed his row
with his brains.

They left him where
he fell to the floor.
We went right on rowing.
Nobody stopping.

Down the captain
sent more to replace him.
From my seat on the bench
I could tell we were moving
but edging ever backward

just barely escaping
the island of flame.
It boiled and popped
and showered us in pebbles.

Each little stone
an offering solution.
A clunky reminder.
If I only had the guts.

Three days we were there
until the fire subsided
and a storm wind blew us off
the scorched patch of ocean.

Our hands looked
like giant black paws.
The captain told us
to urinate on them

to keep down the blisters
and prevent complication
but we were so parched
we hadn't the luxury.

We sat at the base
of our benches in agony.
We'd been hurled off course
from a searing drama

to the slowest
patch of doldrums
our ship had ever squatted.
The sea was molasses

and we, a dying fly.
This time a deckhand
grabbed up a pebble
and stuck it in a board.

He went at his head with it.
Sadly it didn't fire
the first time he tried.
He was getting worse

with each continuing bludgeon.
We were so exhausted
and disturbed
and half dead ourselves

that all we could do
was lie around and watch.
All of a sudden
a shipmate stood up

and peeled the board
from his wretched hand.
He was melting in agony.
His face all but smashed

looking up at him
with one eye swollen
the other closing down fast.
With a pleading shrug

his hands falling open
he kneeled in front
of the man with his board.
That's when the mate

took one sporting whack
and saved the poor life
of the cowering dead man
by firing the explosive

down on his head.
Those who could move
made the cross
on their chest.

Others simply shifted
their eyeballs away
to another angle
of our ghastly hold.

I've had more than enough
of this woesome voyage.
That's why I'm going
to put down my oar.

I saved one of the pebbles
in my shirt for this occasion
and have slid it into
my ear for accuracy.

Now all I need do
is ask the shipmate
with the board
still standing

to please do me
the reasonable honor.
Hopefully he'll get it
on the very first try.

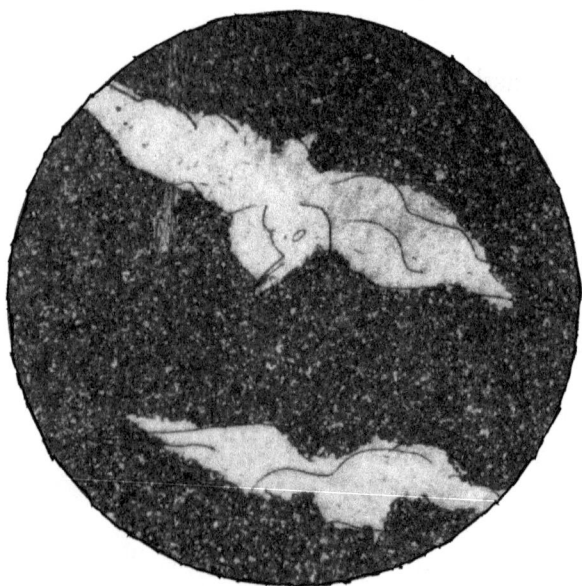

War Lovers

Deep in your bed at night
under the fever of darkness
after the rains have set down
beneath the brace of your covers

the fading call of psyche
as if you're even able.
What will you say to her now
what can you take away?

And after all that war
she never left you with manna.
And if you sleep in the light
you know the moon would avoid you.

I've been lonely now
for over ten thousand years.

If there's a rogue in the world
how can our armies defeat it
and what can War Lovers do
after the guns have erased them?

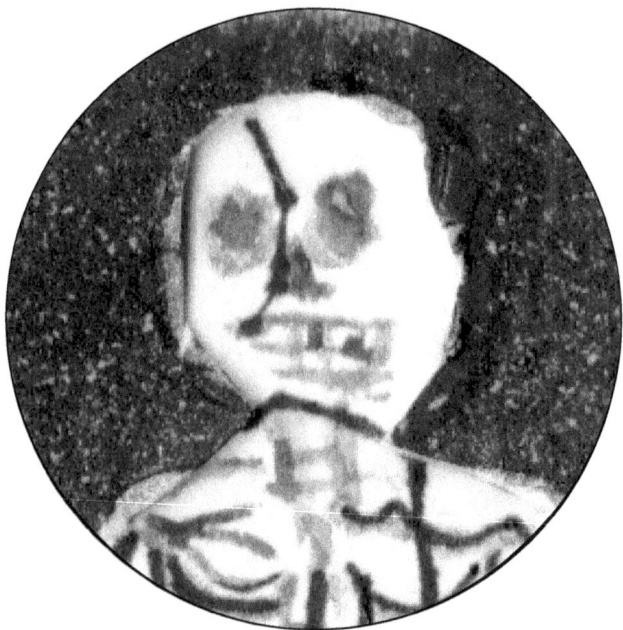

What The Sailor Was Thinking

Today, wind and waves toss the ship.
Another salt-soaked crisis
to shout down the memory
of our former selves.

Yardarms crush our bones
while ropes flail and insult us
and the pong of rum spice mixed
with brine smells to high heaven.

Yet we are still in skin.
Many things keep us here
to roam the undulating deep
fortune, desire, heroism.

And how does a hero win?
Alone.
And how does a hero die?
Alone.

In spite of the odds,
we who abandon any deviation
are destroyed and regenerated
by the wind.

What The Sea Said

Once, an angry ocean folded itself
into a cliff and rose up to speak to me
at the side of the ship where I worked.

It sputtered and grumbled
in anger, showering the deck
with brine and kelp.

I stood aghast to face it.
None of the crew took heed
as they were busy commanding the vessel

through catacombs of fate
in the midst of a third
storm on our voyage.

"You utter fool!"
Spake the heap of sea that soaked my body.

"You senseless blithering automaton!
we are not you nor do we support you!

We ignore you and reject you!
You finless pink blots
tottering about that wooden whale belly!

Those brothers you lost? Each of them deserved it.
The current you seek? It would rather misguide you.

If you try to stand upright I say that balance itself is an illusion!
Here we twist and turn and dump our innards as part of our daily course!

You think you have conquered us but we will betray you.
You brave our expanse in lonely lust, but the horizon will always evade you.

The pale skinned puppets you cry for on shore
would rather have you at their side
and you ought to be with them.

We will see to it that they are flooded
and washed down the river.
For, we are both the clouds and the river
and we will work hard
to force you to quit
your vainglorious explorations.
We would rather remain unknown!"

I let go of the ropes that were bracing me.
The ocean tore open its insides
and pointed to a canyon deep within it.
I bowed my head and followed
without hesitation.

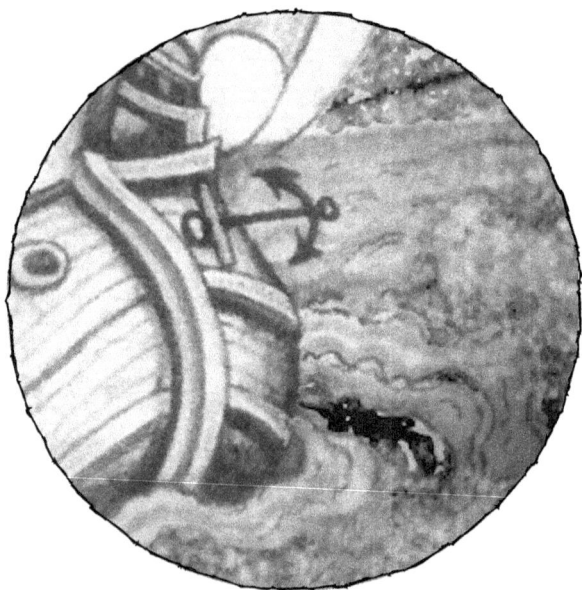

Again she plunges! hark! a second shock
Bilges the splitting vessel on the rock;
Down on the vale of death, with dismal cries,
The fated victims shuddering cast their eyes
In wild despair; while yet another stroke
With strong convulsion rends the solid oak:
Ah Heaven!—behold her crashing ribs divide!
She loosens, parts, and spreads in ruin o'er the tide.

—William Falconer,
The Shipwreck, Canto III, line 642

Wreck of the Europa

Rains of bloodshed over the topsails
brash waves on deck and me waist down
she can no longer bear the effects of our cosseting.
Confusion and lonely death
for vessel-borne wood worshippers.

She who espoused that place
between the sacred pair of wife and mother
thinks not of hammering us to watery hell.
Screams of Europa span her attention
to adjacent ships ripped and foundering
about the rocks

sailors spill shouting, swimming foamy waters,
engrossed.

Captain slogs his fist at the wheel
broad shoulders tremble. From behind,
Anubis swings a beam against him.
That crown propped with a stump-like piling
slips from its joint with a whimper.

Raffish subordinates crowd the fore.
Aft decks lower to the water.
Captain limp, hands clasp the helm in death-lock.
Rain wash and sludge fall through the cabins.
The splendent class slings rope and ladders
for themselves, down into the mayhem.

Some crew, water bloated, dive for silver
in the war-bows and break free or perish
should Chance prick the lucky
with airless lungs and shrinking chest,
ribs cracked against the bilge.

Master displays of fruit, gourd, and meat
provision of all kinds, the splendent leaders
all reaped in high stakes of summer
rise through the table to bob on embroidered linen.
Covetous fingers reaching, blind in the foam.

I hush slumped and drawn into a pit of flotsam.
A sailor's life is a jail forever, if between his ears.

I call the wrath of slimy gods of the deep
to drown me in their hidden water.
Random cannon fire belts the names
into a raging, jowled sky.

ABOUT THE AUTHOR.

Youssef Alaoui Fdili is a Moroccan American Latino. His family and heritage are an endless source of inspiration for his varied, dark, spiritual and carnal writings.

Youssef earned an MFA in Poetics from New College of California, Mission District, San Francisco. There, he studied classical Arabic, Spanish baroque and Moroccan contemporary poetry. He is also well versed in 19th Century literature of the fantastic.

His poetry and fiction have appeared in Exquisite Corpse, Big Bridge, Full of Crow, Cherry Bleeds, 580 Split, Carcinogenic Poetry, Tsunami Books, Dusie Press and Red Fez.

youssefalaoui.tumblr.com